A Hug for a Friend

For:

You deserve a special hug!

From:

A good friend is a special gift from God.

Daffodils by the River Wye: Robbie Hildred

Friendship isn't a big thing –
it's a million little things.

•

Friendship is the poetry of life.

•

Friendships that have stood
the test of time are best,
faces wrinkle,
hair grows grey,
but friendship never will decay!

Anon

Hugging has no unpleasant side effects.
It is completely natural.
There are no batteries to replace.
It's inflation-proof and non-fattening.
It doesn't require monthly payments.
It's non-taxable, non-polluting,
and is, of course, fully refundable.

Anon

Photo: Bruce Shippee

A hug is friendship wrapped in arms.
Anon

The Gardens at Anglesey Abbey: Paul Matthews

The world is round so that friendship may encircle it.

Pierre Teilhard de Chardin
French philosopher and Jesuit priest, 1881–1955

A hug delights and warms and charms,
that must be why God gave us arms!

Anon

Tintagel at Sunset: Janet Hann

The breadth of an old friendship
can be measured in happy
memories and shared adventures.

A reassuring presence,
a light when times are dark,
a hand reaching out,
this is what friendship's all about.

Hugs are the universal medicine.

Anon

Piglet sidled up to Pooh from behind. 'Pooh?' he whispered.
'Yes, Piglet?'
'Nothing,' said Piglet, taking Pooh's hand.
'I just wanted to be sure of you.'

A.A. Milne
Winnie the Pooh, 1882–1956

•

Happiness is an unexpected hug.

Friendship is the source of the greatest pleasures...
without friends even the most agreeable
pursuits become tedious.

Thomas Aquinas
Italian Dominican priest, 1225–1274

Jumping the Waves: Linda Freeman

A hug greases the wheels of the world.

•

A hug is the shortest distance between friends.

Anon

...the LORD will watch over your coming and
going both now and for evermore.

Psalm 121:8 **(NIV)**

Driving through the Dales: Mike Williams

A friend is like a good bra...
Hard to find, supportive, comfortable,
always lifts you up, never lets you down,
and is always close to your heart!

•

Friends are our most valuable support in a
world that is sometimes a little crazy. We
should never take them for granted!

Anon

Iris: Liz Edwards

A cheerful friend is like a sunny day,
spreading brightness all around.

Sir John Lubbock
English astronomer, 1803–1865

•

Friends are like crayons: they have many colours.

Anon

•

Friends are those who nourish the spirit.

Anon

•

Friends come and friends go, but a true friend
sticks by you like family.
Proverbs 18:24, The Message

Daisies: Liz Edwards

Twin Fuchsias: Mary Hallett

What is a friend?
A single soul in two bodies.

Aristotle
Greek philosopher, 384–322 BC

•

Friendship doubles the enjoyment
of every shared adventure.

Anon

•

It takes a long time to grow
an old friend.

Anon

•

One loyal friend is worth
ten thousand relatives.

Euripides
Greek playwright, 480–406 BC

A definition of friendship in one word would be... needed!

William Blake
English poet, 1757–1827

•

The glory of friendship is not the outstretched hand,
nor the kindly smile, nor the joy of companionship;
it is the spiritual inspiration that comes to one
when he discovers that someone else believes
in him and is willing to trust him.

Ralph Waldo Emerson
American poet, 1803–1882

Can we be friends?: Liz Edwards

Tulips: Liz Edwards

Joy increases as you give it,
and diminishes as you try to keep it for yourself.
In giving it, you will accumulate a deposit of joy
greater than you ever believed possible.

Norman Vincent Peale
American minister and author, 1898–1993

●

Friends are a joy to the heart.

Anon

You can't wrap love in a box,
but you can wrap a friend in a hug.

Anon

•

You can't give a hug without getting a hug.

Anon

•

I love hugging. I wish I was an octopus,
so I could hug ten people at a time.

Drew Barrymore
American actress, 1975–present day

•

Everybody needs a hug,
it changes your metabolism.

Leo Buscaglia
*American professor and writer,
1924–1998*

Time for Tea...

Tolerance,
Equality and
Acceptance.

It's always TEA time
with my friends...
Anon

Tea for Two: Tim Sandall

Friendship is the only
rose without thorns.

Madeleine de Scudéry
French writer, 1607–1701

Many people will walk in and out
of your life, but only true friends
leave footprints in your heart.

Eleanor Roosevelt
First Lady of the United States, 1884–1962

A kiss without a hug is like a flower
without the fragrance.

Old proverb

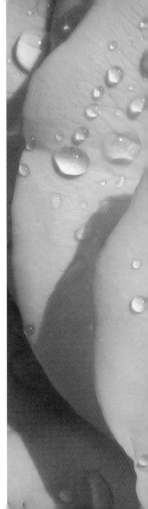

Raindrops on Roses: Rachel Chown

Friendship lifts life to a new level.

•

Hugs are always uplifting.

•

True friends are the folk who never leave your heart, even if they leave your life for a while.

Anon

Hot-Air Balloon: Jean Harvey

Photo: Gale Verhague

A hug can say so many things...

It's great to see you.

I've been missing you.

Thanks for being my friend.

I want you to know how much I care.

Thanks for being there for me.

A hug is a great gift – one size fits all
and it's easy to exchange.

Anon

•

A hug is a handshake from the heart.

Anon

•

A hug is a smile with arms,
a laugh with a stronger grip.

Terri Guillemets
American anthologist, 1973–present day

•

A hug is like a boomerang – you get
it back right away.

Bil Keane
American cartoonist, 1922–present day

Penguin pals: James Groundwater

A true friend is always happy to listen,
and then to listen some more…

A true friend wants nothing more from you
than the pleasure of your company.
Anon

A Quiet Whisper: Ian Strachan

Pigeons on the Prom: Liz Edwards

A friend is someone that you sit with for a quick chat, only to check your watch moments later to find two hours have flown by.

Anon

•

A friend is someone who knows the song of your heart and can always sing it back when you've forgotten the words.

Anon

•

Do not protect yourself by a fence, but rather by your friends.

Czech proverb

A phone call from a far-away friend is like
a hug on your doorstep.

Anon

•

Best friends can always 'catch up' no matter
how many weeks pass without contact.

Anon

•

The language of friends is not words but meanings.

Henry David Thoreau
American writer, 1817–1862

Snowy Telephone Boxes: Liz Edwards

Spring at Anglesey Abbey: Paul Matthews

Friends are the flowers in the garden of life.

Anon

•

It is better to be in chains with friends
than to be in a garden with strangers.

Persian proverb

If you are trusted and people will allow you to
share their inner garden, what better gift?

Fred Rogers
American television presenter and
Presbyterian minister, 1928–2003

A good friend is a special blessing from God
and I thank Him for our friendship.
May God walk with you today and always.
Anon

PS: Never wait until tomorrow to hug someone
you could hug today, because when you give one,
you get one back right away!